STAYING POWER

Motivational Insight To Help You Stay In The Game

by

Van Crouch

Much success!
Van

HONOR BOOKS

Tulsa, Oklahoma

All Scripture quotation is taken from the *King James Version* of the Bible.

2nd Printing

Staying Power
Motivational Insight To Help You Stay In The Game
ISBN 1-56292-228-9
Copyright © 1996 by William V. Crouch
P.O. Box 320
Wheaton, Il. 60187

Published by Honor Books, Inc.
P.O. Box 55388
Tulsa, Oklahoma 74155

INTRODUCTION

Does fear have you paralyzed? Are you afraid to take risks and explore new ventures? Have you become convinced that success comes easily to others but eludes you? Has adversity driven you to the point of giving up?

There are those times in our lives when we wake up and realize that we're not the success we had planned to be. Problems seem to pile upon problems, worries upon worries, and fear begins to set in. Sleep comes less easily, tears begin to flow more frequently, and you and I may wonder, does anybody really care?

I know these feelings because I've been there too. At some point in our lives, we all come to a point of genuine testing or a period of despair. It might be the break-up of a marriage, the loss of a job, a serious illness, or the death of a loved one. It's a time that can cause a person to become bitter or better. Why do some people grow despondent and quit, while others refuse to let tough times defeat them?

How can you get up when you've been knocked down? What can you do when all seems lost? Why is it that some people manage to turn their problems into possibilities? Some seem to grow through tough times, learn from them, and overcome overwhelming odds to step back on the path of success, happiness, and hope.

In this book I have compiled a collection of quotes for those times of adversity we all face — when we don't feel we can run another step, fight another round, or play another quarter. Here is the insight and inspiration you need to build new dreams from the ashes of defeat.

Your failure is not fatal. Your defeat is not final. Your problem has a limited life span. So go ahead and get up! Dust yourself off! There's **STAYING POWER** on the inside of you and it's too soon to quit!

Van Crouch

**I can accept failure,
everyone fails at something.
But I can't accept not trying.**

Michael Jordan

**A Hollywood producer
scrawled a rejection note
on a manuscript that became
Gone With The Wind.**

Anonymous

5

The minute you start talking about what you're going to do if you lose, you have lost.

George Shultz

If it had not been for the wind in my face, I wouldn't be able to fly at all.

Arthur Ashe

**I always did my best when
I realized the assignment
was going to be difficult.
From there, my attitude
was better, more serious,
and I got down to the job of
preparing myself better than if I
thought it was going to be easy.**

Ted Williams

Go as far as you can see, and when you get there, you will see farther.

Anonymous

A winner is someone who recognizes his God-given talents, works his tail off to develop them into skills, and uses these skills to accomplish his goals.

Larry Bird

The reason a guy like myself has achieved some success in life is that I've worked very, very hard to do so.

Tony Dorsett

Every time I stepped on the field, I believed my team was going to walk off the winner, somehow, some way.

Roger Staubach

The key to any game is to use your strengths and hide your weaknesses.

Paul Westphal

There are no victories at bargain prices.

General Dwight D. Eisenhower

You hit home runs not by chance, but by preparation.

Roger Maris

When you've got something to prove, there's nothing greater than a challenge.

Terry Bradshaw

Do you know what my favorite part of the game is? The opportunity to play. It is as simple as that. ...I love that opportunity.

Mike Singletary

If it weren't for the dark days, we wouldn't know what it is to walk in the light.

Earl Campbell

I don't think anything is unrealistic if you believe you can do it. I think if you are determined enough and willing to pay the price, you can get it done.

Mike Ditka

> **Problems are the price you pay for progress.**
>
> *Branch Rickey*

> **I want to be remembered as the guy who gave his all whenever he was on the field. I want people to know that I was putting out on every play.**
>
> *Walter Payton*

I don't seem able to do my best unless I'm behind or in trouble.

Mildred "Babe" Didrikson Zaharias

I play to win, whether during practice or a real game. And I will not let anything get in the way of me and my competitive enthusiasm to win.

Michael Jordan

Once you say you're going to settle for second, that's what happens to you in life, I find.

John F. Kennedy

There is no substitute for effort. Always play up to your full potential in every endeavor. The greatest extravagance of all is to waste human potential.

Joe Robbie

If winning isn't important, why do they keep score?

Adolph Rupp

To finish first you must first finish.

Rick Mears

Leave as little to chance as possible. Preparation is the key to success.

Paul Brown

Don't be afraid to take a big step. You can't cross a chasm in two small jumps.

David Lloyd George

If you deliberately plan to be less than you are capable of being, then I warn you that you'll be unhappy for the rest of your life.

Abraham Maslow

If people knew how hard I worked to get my mastery, it wouldn't seem so wonderful after all.

Michelangelo

You have enormous untapped power that you will probably never tap, because most people never run far enough on their first wind to ever find they have a second.

William James

**Everything comes to him
who hustles while he waits.**

Thomas Edison

**A man is not hurt so much by what
happens, as by his opinion of what
happens.**

Michel de Montaigne

**You don't have any problems.
All you need is faith in God!**

R.W. Schambach

**Success seems to be largely a matter of
hanging on after others have let go.**

William Feather

The atmosphere of expectancy is the breeding ground for miracles.

Rodney L. Parsley

There's no such thing as coulda, shoulda and woulda. If you shoulda and coulda, you woulda done it.

Pat Riley

**The only thing that stands
between a man and what he
wants from life is often merely
the will to try it and the faith
to believe that it is possible.**

Richard M. Devos

The best way to escape from a problem is to solve it.

Anonymous

Success is never final and failure never fatal. It's courage that counts.

George F. Tilton

You don't have to be a fantastic hero to do certain things — to compete. You can be just an ordinary chap, sufficiently motivated to reach challenging goals.

Sir Edmund Hillary

Never complain about what you permit.

Mike Murdock

Nothing in the world can take the place of persistence.

Calvin Coolidge

There are people in show business who became major stars simply because they didn't have sense enough to quit when they should have.

Bertrand Russell

The most tragic of all, in the long run, is the ultimate attitude; it doesn't matter.

Rollo May

Mistakes are easy, mistakes are inevitable, but there is no mistake so great as the mistake of not going on.

William Blake

Nothing good comes in life or athletics unless a lot of hard work has preceded the effort. Only temporary success is achieved by taking short cuts.

Roger Staubach

Success is getting up just one more time than you fall down.

Doc Blakely

Never give up, for that is just the place and time that the tide will turn.

Harriet Beecher Stowe

Management by objectives works if you know the objectives. Ninety percent of the time you don't.

Peter Drucker

If you don't have enough pride, you're going to get beat every play.

Gale Sayers

Failure is the opportunity to begin again, more intelligently.

Henry Ford

34

Show me a thoroughly satisfied man, and I will show you a failure.

Thomas Edison

When you're through improving you're through.

Rick Warren

I never quit trying. I never felt that I didn't have a chance to win.

Arnold Palmer

There is no education like adversity.

Benjamin Disraeli

**Failing doesn't make you
a failure. Giving up,
accepting your failure,
refusing to try again, does!**

Richard Exley

The only yardstick for success our society has is being a champion. No one remembers anything else.

John Madden

I don't know the key to success, but the key to failure is trying to please everybody.

Bill Cosby

People fail in direct proportion to their willingness to accept socially acceptable excuses for failure.

W. Steven Brown

I will go anywhere as long as it's forward.

David Livingston

Winning is a habit. Unfortunately, so is losing.

Vince Lombardi

One of the things I learned the hard way was that it doesn't pay to get discouraged. Keeping busy and making optimism a way of life can restore your faith in yourself.

Lucille Ball

Nobody ever drowned in his own sweat.

Ann Landers

I feel every person can have everything if they are willing to work, work, work.

Estee Lauder

Nobody should think they can just coast through life on the basis of gifts that they have nothing to do with in the first place. You have to pay your dues and do your homework.

Steve Allen

No man is a fool to give up
what he cannot keep to gain
what he cannot lose.

Jim Elliot

The last of the human freedoms is to
choose one's attitude in any given set
of circumstances.

Victor Frankl

There's a difference between interest and commitment. When you're interested in doing something, you do it only when it's convenient. When you're committed to something, you accept no excuses, only results.

Kenneth Blanchard

The important thing to remember is that if you don't have that inspired enthusiasm that is contagious — whatever you do have is also contagious.

Danny Cox

Turn your losses into a plus. I think if you approach it right, you can turn every setback you have into an advantage.

George Allen

Champions are a rare breed. They trust God while others ask for answers. They step forward while everyone else prays for volunteers. They see beyond the dangers, the risks, the obstacles, and the hardships.

Lester Sumrall

There has always been something new, demanding and testing every day I play. I love the challenge.

Nancy Lopez

I didn't want to quit and say for the rest of my life, "Well maybe I could have been..."

Frank Shorter

The spirit, the will to win, and the will to excel are the things that endure. These qualities are so much more important than the events that occur.

Vince Lombardi

I don't meet the competition.
I crush it.

Charles Revson

The more difficult a victory,
the greater the happiness in winning.

Pele

You can't get much done in life if you
only work on the days
when you feel good.

Jerry West

Consistency is what counts;
you have to be able to
do things over and over again.

Hank Aaron

51

Don't look back.
Someone might be gaining on you.

Satchel Paige

My ambition is not to be
just a good fighter. I want to
be great, something special.

Sugar Ray Leonard

When you make a mistake, there are only three things you should ever do about it:
1. Admit it
2. Learn from it, and
3. Don't repeat it.

Paul "Bear" Bryant

A winner never whines.

Paul Brown

It's not so important who starts the game, but who finishes it.

John Wooden

It's great to win, but it's also great fun just to be in the thick of any truly well and hard-fought contest against opponents you respect, whatever the outcome.

Jack Nicklaus

You just can't beat the person who never gives up.

Babe Ruth

If you keep doing what you've always done, you'll keep getting what you've always got.

Peter Francisco

**I always felt that I hadn't
achieved what I wanted
to achieve. I always felt
I could get better.
That's the whole incentive.**

Virginia Wade

Don't over-react to the trouble makers.

Warren Bennis

He who has a "why" to live for can bear almost any "how."

Nietzsche

Success is never final.

Winston Churchill

If a man hasn't discovered something that he will die for, he isn't fit to live.

Martin Luther King, Jr.

Never let what you cannot do interfere
with what you can do.

John Wooden

The real glory is being knocked to your
knees and then coming back. That's
real glory. That's the essence of it.

Vince Lombardi

Life owes us little; we owe it everything. The only true happiness comes from squandering ourselves for a purpose.

John Marm Brown

God will not look you over for medals, degrees or diplomas, but for scars.

Elbert Hubbard

Those who stand for nothing may fall for anything.

Alexander Hamilton

As you get older, don't slow down; speed up. There's less time left.

Malcolm Forbes

You may occasionally give out — but never give up.

Mary Crowley

Blessed are those who expect nothing, for they shall not be disappointed.

Jonathan Swift

The road to success has many tempting parking places.

Steve Potter

The winds blow strongest against those who stand tallest.

F.C. Hayes

Quitting is a permanent solution to a temporary situation.

Dr. Rob Gilbert

Anything I've ever done that ultimately was worth while...initially scared me to death.

Betty Bender

A great pleasure in life is doing what people say you cannot do.

Walter Gagebot

Take risks. You can't fall off the bottom.

Barbara Proctor

The moment you commit and quit holding back, all sorts of unforeseen incidents, meetings and material assistance will rise up to help you. The simple act of commitment is a powerful magnet for help.

Napoleon Hill

When all is said and done, as a rule, more is said than done.

Lou Holtz

You can become a winner only if you are willing to walk over the edge.

Damon Runyon

You can either take action, or you can hang back and hope for a miracle. Miracles are great, but they are so unpredictable.

Peter Drucker

People who never get carried away should be.

Malcolm Forbes

For every obstacle there is a solution over, under, around or through.

Dan Zadra

I believe that genius is an infinite capacity for taking life by the scruff of the neck.

Christopher Quill

Do the thing and you will have the power.

Emerson

Others can stop you temporarily; only you can do it permanently.

Don Ward

**There is only one you.
God wanted you to be you.
Don't you dare change just
because you're outnumbered!**

Charles Swindoll

The world is an oyster, but you don't crack it open on a mattress.

Arthur Miller

A year from now you may wish you had started today.

Karen Lamb

We must have courage to bet on our ideas, to take the calculated risk, and to act. Everyday living requires courage if life is to be effective and bring happiness.

Maxwell Maltz

Amateurs hope.
Professionals make it happen.

Garson Kanin

Besides pride, loyalty, discipline,
heart and mind, confidence is the
key to all the locks.

Joe Paterno

Never mistake motion for action.

Ernest Hemingway

No matter what the statistics say, there's always a way.

Bernard Siegel

It is a rough road that leads to the heights of greatness.

Seneca

There is nothing so fatiguing as the eternal hanging on of an uncompleted task.

William James

If one advances confidently in the direction of his dreams, and endeavors to live the life which he has imagined, he will meet with success unexpected in common hours.

Henry David Thoreau

It is only in our decisions that we are important.

Jean-Paul Sartre

Being on the tightrope is living; everything else is waiting.

Karl Wallenda

Wherever you see a successful business, someone once made a courageous decision.

Peter Drucker

Morale is the state of mind. It is steadfastness and courage and hope.

General George Marshall

Great men are meteors designed to burn so that earth may be lighted.

Napoleon Bonaparte

The best way to cheer yourself up is to cheer everybody else up.

Mark Twain

Ain't no chance if you don't take it.

Guy Clark

For every pass I ever caught in a game, I caught a thousand in practice.

Don Hutson

**If you're knocked down,
you can't lose your guts.
You need to play with
supreme confidence or else
you'll lose again, and then
losing becomes a habit.**

Joe Paterno

Failure is never final and success is never-ending. Success is a journey, not a destination.

Dr. Robert Schuller

Push yourself again and again... don't give an inch until the final buzzer sounds.

Larry Bird

The force of selfishness is as inevitable and as calculable as the force of gravitation.

Hailliard

If at first you don't succeed, you are running about average.

M.H. Alderson

In war there is no substitute for victory.

Douglas MacArthur

Winners are just ex-losers who got mad. The battle belongs to the persistent. The victory will go to the one who does not quit! Refuse to let friends or circumstances defeat you.

Van Crouch

Men die of fright and live of confidence.

Henry David Thoreau

Impossible is a word to be found only in the dictionary of fools.

Napoleon Bonaparte

There is no finish line.

Nike Corporation

When in doubt, risk it.

Holbrook Jackson

Show me a good and gracious loser, and I'll show you a failure.

Knute Rockne

If you risk nothing, then you risk everything.

Geena Davis

If a man does his best,
what else is there?

George S. Patton

The man who complains about
the way the ball bounces is likely
the one who dropped it.

Lou Holtz

I have fought a good fight, I have finished my course, I have kept the faith.

2 Timothy 4:7

**Take your job seriously but
learn to laugh at yourself.**

Don Ward

**If you aren't fired with enthusiasm,
you will be fired with enthusiasm.**

Vince Lombardi

Lord, deliver me from the man who never makes a mistake, and also from the man who makes the same mistake twice.

Dr. William J. Mayo

Failure is the path of least persistence.

Anonymous

What I do is prepare myself until I know I can do what I have to do.

Joe Namath

Everyone has an obligation as well as the privilege of leading in something. Leadership begins with a simple decision to pay the price and ends the moment you cease to pay it. The price: Loneliness, weariness, abandonment, vision.

Charles E. Jones

**Problems can become opportunities
when the right people come together.**

Robert Redford

**The world is full of willing people;
some willing to work,
the others willing to let them.**

Robert Frost

Winners can tell you where they are going, what they plan to do along the way and who will be sharing the adventure with them.

Denis Waitley

I've never seen a monument
erected to a pessimist.

Paul Harvey

The man who follows the crowd
will never be followed by a crowd.

John Maxwell

You're not finished when you're defeated . . . you're finished when you quit.

Van Crouch

A man is only as big as he thinks he is. There's no limit on what you can do.

Ben Feldman

Nobody remembers who came in second.

Charles Schulz

You're a hero when you win and a bum when you lose. That's the game.

Johnny Unitas

**If you think you can win, you can win.
Faith is necessary to victory.**

William Hazlitt

**Every time you win, you're reborn;
when you lose, you die a little.**

George Allen

One machine can do the work of fifty ordinary men. No machine can do the work of one extraordinary man.

Elbert Hubbard

I wondered why somebody didn't do something; then I realized that I was somebody.

Anonymous

Your attitude, not your aptitude, will determine your altitude.

Zig Ziglar

Human beings can alter their lives by altering their attitudes.

William James

You either emulate the faults or virtues of parents or you turn them around — reverse them.

Charles F. Luce

Leadership is not a right — it's a responsibility.

John Maxwell

I don't see any virtue in losing. This society rewards people who win.

Robert Crandall

The habit of looking on the best side of every event is worth more than a thousand pounds a year.

Samuel Johnson

To avoid criticism, do nothing, say nothing, be nothing.

Elbert Hubbard

The key to successful leadership today is influence, not authority.

Kenneth Blanchard

A leader is one who knows the way, goes the way, and shows the way.

John Maxwell

All glory comes from daring to begin.

Eugene F. Ware

You can't build a reputation on what you're going to do.

Henry Ford

The most pathetic person in the world is someone who has sight but has no vision.

Helen Keller

Leadership is both something you are, and something you do.

Fred Smith

Even if you're on the right track, you'll get run over if you just sit there.

Will Rogers

The fullness or emptiness of life will be measured by the extent to which a man feels that he has an impact on the lives of others. To be a man is to matter to someone outside yourself, or to some calling or cause bigger than yourself.

Kingman Brewster

The only thing harder to handle than winning too much is losing too much.

John Wooden

The task of the leader is to get his people from where they are to where they have not been.

Henry Kissinger

Why are there so many best-sellers about how to dress or plan or eat for success — and so few on how to work for it?

Arch Napier

I do not believe in defeat.

Bill Hartack

Victory is everything. You can spend the money, but you can never spend the memories.

Ken Venturi

Confidence doesn't come out of nowhere. It's a result of something...hours and days and weeks and years of constant work and dedication.

Roger Staubach

When you win nothing hurts.

Joe Namath

You have to know you can win.
You have to think you can win.
You have to feel you can win.

Sugar Ray Leonard

No one ever accomplishes anything of consequence without a goal...Goal setting is the strongest human force for self-motivation.

Paul Myer

Winning breeds confidence and confidence breeds winning.

Hubert Green

If you start worrying about the people in the stands, before too long you're in the stands with them.

Tommy Lasorda

My mother taught me very early to believe I could achieve any accomplishment I wanted to. The first was to walk without braces.

Wilma Rudolph

They say I teach brutal football, the only thing brutal about football is losing.

Paul "Bear" Bryant

To repeat successes of the past, you follow your old program. Don't get fancy; just be consistent.

Bill Rodgers

I rely on two important qualities to win — discipline and concentration. Then I concentrate totally on playing my game and on winning.

Tracy Austin

You've got to take the initiative
and play your game. Confidence
makes the difference.

Chris Evert

If there was just one word I could use
to describe a successful person,
that one word would be attitude.

Bart Starr

On the ice I'm aggressive.
To race is to go all out, every
time, no matter what happens.
I never worry about falling.

Bonnie Blair

If you do not think about the future, you cannot have one.

John Gale

I've always believed that anybody with a little ability, a little guts and the desire to apply himself can make it.

Willie Shoemaker

> When you come to a fork
> in the road, take it.
>
> *Yogi Berra*

> To be a leader, you have to make people
> want to follow you, and nobody wants
> to follow someone who doesn't
> know where he's going.
>
> *Joe Namath*

A person always doing his or her best becomes a natural leader, just by example.

Joe DiMaggio

Many people resented my impatience and honesty, but I never cared about acceptance as much as I cared about respect.

Jackie Robinson

There is an intensity and a danger in football — as in life generally — which keeps us alive and awake. It is a test of our awareness and ability. Like so much of life, it presents us with the choice of responding with fear or with action.

John Brodie

If you don't have a dream, how can you have a dream come true?

Faye LaPointe

The secret of winning football games is working more as a team, less as individuals. I play not my eleven best, but my best eleven.

Knute Rockne

Show me a boy or girl with a desire to win, and I'll show you a person who will work hard the thousands of hours it takes to win. If they lack desire, they won't work.

Bob Richards

When you're through changing, you're through.

Bruce Barton

Lord, grant that I may always desire more than I can accomplish.

Michelangelo

**I learned that the only way
you are going to get anywhere
in life is to work hard at it.
If you do, you'll win —
if you don't you won't.**

Bruce Jenner

Don't pray for dreams equal to your powers. Pray for powers equal to your dreams.

Michael Nolan

Great minds have purposes; others have wishes.

Washington Irving

A #2 pencil and a dream can take you anywhere.

J. Meyers

Every thought is a seed. If you plant crab apples, don't count on harvesting Golden Delicious.

Bill Meyer

141

Whatever you're ready for is ready for you.

Mark Victor Hansen

The best minute you spend is the one you invest in people.

Blanchard and Johnson

The real winners in life are the people who look at every situation with an expectation that they can make it work or make it better.

Barbara Pletcher

Care enough for a result, and you will almost certainly attain it.

William James

There is no such thing as a minor lapse of integrity.

Tom Peters

Act as if what you do
makes a difference. It does.

William James

It's a funny thing about life. If you
refuse to accept anything
but the best, you very often get it.

Somerset Maugham

There is no traffic jam on the extra mile.

Business Axiom

Enthusiasm is contagious. Start an epidemic.

Don Ward

The greatest crime in
the world is not developing
your potential. When you
do what you do best,
you are helping others.

Roger Williams

Enthusiasm is faith set on fire.

George Adams

Prepare.
The time to win your battle
is before it starts.

Frederick W. Lewis

**The real friend of his country
is the person who believes
in excellence, seeks for it,
fights for it, defends it,
and tries to produce it.**

Morley Callaghan

Formula for success: Underpromise and overdeliver.

Tom Peters

Anyone with a new idea is a crank —
until the idea succeeds.

Mark Twain

A good plan vigorously executed right
now is far better than a perfect plan
executed next week.

General George Patton

No, you never get any fun out of things
you haven't done.

Ogden Nash

As you grow older, you'll find the only
things you regret are
the things you didn't do.

Zachary Scott

A wise leader resolves conflicts peaceably, not forcibly.

Anonymous

Cause something to happen.

Paul "Bear" Bryant

Why go into something to test the waters? Go into it to make waves.

Michael Nolan

If you ain't the lead dog, the scenery never changes.

Buddy Ryan

The privilege of a lifetime is being who you are.

Joseph Campbell

The graveyards are full of indispensable men.

Charles de Gaulle

Give what you have. To someone, it may be better than you dare to think.

Henry Wadsworth Longfellow

To be prepared is half the victory.

Miguel de Cervantes

Power is not revealed
by striking hard or often,
but by striking true.

Honoré de Balzac

You are about to experience a turning point. Stay in the game — it's too soon to quit!

Van Crouch

ABOUT THE AUTHOR

Van Crouch is widely regarded as one of the best and more versatile speakers in America. As the founder and president of the consulting firm, Van Crouch Communications, Van challenges individuals to achieve excellence in their lives.

Ranked as a consistent sales leader with the American Express Company, Van went on to receive many awards for outstanding performance in the insurance industry and has been a qualifying member of the Million Dollar Round Table.

Van Crouch authored the best-selling books, *Stay In The Game* and *Winning 101*, and is in demand for his thought-provoking seminars and keynote engagements to Fortune 500 companies, government organizations, professional sports teams, church groups, and management and sales conventions worldwide.

Van Crouch has the ability to motivate people to raise their level of expectation. He is sure to both inspire and challenge you.

Van Crouch Communications
P.O. Box 320
Wheaton, Il. 60187

Additional copies of this book and other portable titles from
Honor Books are available at your local bookstore.

Winning 101 by Van Crouch
God's Little Instruction Book series by Honor Books
The Making of A Champion by Mike Murdock
Momentum Builders by John Mason
How To Be an Up Person in a Down World by Honor Books
Don't Wait For Your Ship to Come In by Honor Books